Pioneers in science, technology, engineering, and math

TRAILBLAZERS OF TECHNOLOGY

Rob Colson

CRABTREE
PUBLISHING COMPANY
WWW.CRABTREEBOOKS.COM

Published in Canada
Crabtree Publishing
616 Welland Avenue
St. Catharines, ON
L2M 5V6

Published in the United States
Crabtree Publishing
PMB 59051
350 Fifth Ave, 59th Floor
New York, NY 10118

Published in 2019 by Crabtree Publishing Company

First Published in Great Britain in 2018 by Wayland
Copyright © Hodder and Stoughton, 2018

Author: Rob Colson

Editorial director: Kathy Middleton

Editors: Elise Short, Wendy Scavuzzo

Proofreader: Ellen Rodger

Designer: Ben Ruocco

Prepress technician: Ken Wright

Print coordinator: Katherine Berti

The website addresses (URLs) included in this book were valid at the time of going to press. However, it is possible that contents or addresses may have changed since the publication of this book. No responsibility for any such changes can be accepted by either the author or the Publisher.

Images:
t–top, b–bottom, l–left, r–right, c–center,
front cover–fc, back cover–bc
All images courtesy of Dreamstime.com and all icons made by Freepik from www.flaticon.com, unless indicated

Inside front Elena11/Shutterstock;; fc, bc Deviney; fcr, 12-13 Ezumeimages; fcbl Scanrail; fcbl Aprescindere; fcbl, 26br Leonardo255; bcl, 12bl Library of Congress; bcl, 22cl MGM/ Clarence Bull; bcl, 14cr Library and Archives Canada; 4–5 Johns Hopkins University Applied Physics Laboratory; 5br Grendelkhan/ Attribution-ShareAlike 4.0 International (CC BY-SA 4.0); 6-7 Olegdudko; 7tr 22tomtom; 8c Vvostal; 9br Ivansmuk; 9br Valery Lisin; 10br Aprescindere; 11tr Everett Collection Inc.; 14bl National Archives and Records Administration; 14-15 Cowardlion; 15br Jiripravda; 17b Smashicons; 19t Pattarapong Kumlert; 20l Library of Congress; 20br Hzeller/Attribution-ShareAlike 3.0 Unported (CC BY-SA 3.0); 21t Mikhail Basov; 21t Sswartz; 22–23 Dvmsimages; 24bl Enrique Dans/ Attribution 2.0 Generic (CC BY 2.0); 24–25 Pressureua; 26bl Redrum0486/Attribution-ShareAlike 3.0 Unported (CC BY-SA 3.0); 26bc Dmitry Kazantsev; 26cr Joseph Brophy; 27bl Krystyna Wojciechowska – Czarnik; 28bl US Naval Research Laboratory; 28–29 NOAA; 29t Andrey Yaroslavtsev/Shutterstock; 29br marrishuanna/Shutterstock; 31br Reservoir Dots/Shutterstock.

Every effort has been made to acknowledge every image source but the publisher apologizes for any unintentional errors or omissions that will be corrected in future editions of this book.

Printed in the U.S.A./122018/CG20181005

Library and Archives Canada Cataloguing in Publication

Colson, Rob, 1971-, author
    Trailblazers of technology / Rob Colson.

(STEM-gineers)
Includes index.
Issued in print and electronic formats.
ISBN 978-0-7787-5739-9 (hardcover).--
ISBN 978-0-7787-5825-9 (softcover).--
ISBN 978-1-4271-2236-0 (HTML)

    1. Technology--History--Juvenile literature. 2. Technological innovations--Juvenile literature. 3. Technology--Experiments--Juvenile literature. 4. Inventors--Biography--Juvenile literature. I. Title.

T48.C655 2018   j609   C2018-905458-1
                                    C2018-905459-X

Library of Congress Cataloging-in-Publication Data

Names: Colson, Rob, author.
Title: Trailblazers of technology / Rob Colson.
Description: New York, New York : Crabtree Publishing Company, 2019. | Series: STEM-gineers | Includes index.
Identifiers: LCCN 2018043640 (print) | LCCN 2018049431 (ebook) | ISBN 9781427122360 (Electronic) | ISBN 9780778757399 (hardcover) | ISBN 9780778758259 (pbk.)
Subjects: LCSH: Telecommunication--Juvenile literature. | Electrical engineering--Juvenile literature. | Engineers--Biography--Juvenile literature. | Inventors--Biography--Juvenile literature.
Classification: LCC TK5102.4 (ebook) | LCC TK5102.4 J66 2019 (print) | DDC 621.3092/2--dc23
LC record available at https://lccn.loc.gov/2018043640

CONTENTS

TECHNOLOGY
RULES THE WORLD

All kinds of technologies have been created to help people do work. The first technologies were simple tools made by hand by one or two people. Modern technologies often require thousands of people to make them. Some are designed with and run by computers to perform tasks that would have been unimaginable just a few decades ago.

Simple machines

The earliest technologies were in the form of six tools we call simple **machines**. These machines make work easier by changing the size or direction of a force, such as a push or a pull. They help a person do the same work with less effort.

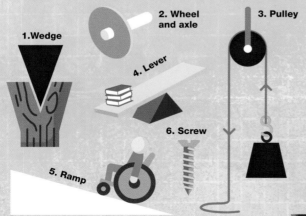

1. Wedge
2. Wheel and axle
3. Pulley
4. Lever
5. Ramp
6. Screw

Ancient technology

Many of the earliest technologies were developed to help farmers. The Archimedes screw was invented 3,000 years ago by the Greek **engineer** Archimedes. The screw raises water from a stream up the bank into fields to help crops grow. As the screw is turned, water is scooped up at the bottom and pushed up along the screw's spiral through a tube to the field. Farmers still use Archimedes screws today.

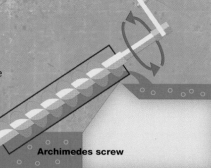

Archimedes screw

Digital revolution

Modern technologies are driven by computers, which are constantly being improved. Computers do not only control machines, they can also design them.

Human and machine

Robotic arms and legs were designed for people who have lost limbs through illness or accidents. A developing technology for robotic limbs allows them to be attached to nerves that lead to the brain. The wearer can then control the limb with their thoughts.

The present and the future

Computer technology has created a new generation of machines that can learn from experience. Self-driving cars have only recently been introduced on public roads. With each journey, self-driving cars learn from each new situation they face. They can update their systems to show the best course of action to take if the same situation happens again. In the future, this technology could save many lives by reducing accidents.

Google's Waymo driverless car finds its way using a system called Lidarl. It bounces laser beams off nearby objects to tell how close the car is to them.

Read on to discover the technological challenges inventors have overcome. The answers to each project's questions are found on page 31.

CREATING A CURRENT

A battery is a storage device for energy created from chemicals. A battery produces an electric current when it is linked up to a **circuit**. The first battery was made in 1800 by Italian inventor Alessandro Volta.

Alessandro Volta (1745–1827)

Volta made his battery by building up layers of zinc and copper, separated by cloth soaked in saltwater. When he connected the top and bottom of his battery with a wire, an electric current flowed through it. Named after its inventor, the first battery was known as a voltaic pile.

Volta's battery used cells of zinc, copper, and saltwater to create an electric charge.

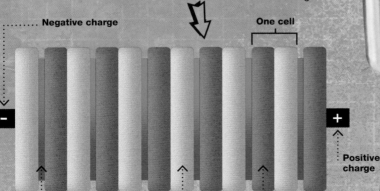

Negative charge

One cell

−

+

Positive charge

Saltwater   Zinc   Copper

How did it work?

Back then, Volta did not fully understand how his battery worked. Electricity is created by the flow of tiny particles called **electrons**. In a battery, a flow of electrons is created when the metals and chemicals contained in it react to one another. A battery has one positive terminal, or end, and one negative terminal. The electrons flow in one direction from the negative end of the battery, through a circuit, and back to the positive end of the battery. In Volta's battery, a chemical reaction between the zinc and the saltwater produced a negative charge in the zinc plate. Electrons entered the saltwater at the copper plate. This set up a flow of electrons through a wire connecting the zinc plate to the copper plate.

Modern batteries follow the same basic principle as the voltaic pile.

Recharging

A battery can be recharged, or refilled with energy, by reversing the chemical reaction in the battery. Electrons will flow toward the negative terminal instead of the positive terminal, restoring the battery's power. Some electric cars can travel more than 300 miles (482 km) on one charge. Their batteries can be plugged into on-street charging points, or stations.

pROJECT: ICE CUBE TRAY BATTERY

Power an LED with this homemade battery.

You will need: an ice cube tray, five galvanized (zinc coated) nails, five pieces of copper wire, distilled vinegar, and an **LED** (light-emitting diode)

1. Wrap one piece of wire around the top of each nail so some wire hangs down the side.

2. Fill the first six cells of the ice cube tray with vinegar. Straddle the LED across the first two cells.

3. Place a nail in one of the first two cells, and have the copper wire dip into the next cell. Place the next nail in that cell and drape the wire into the next cell. Repeat until the last piece of copper dips into the cell with the LED.

The LED should light up. If you have more nails and wire, try using more of the cells to make a battery. Does the LED shine brighter?

CAPTURING AN IMAGE

Photographs capture images of the world for us to look at forever. Photographic technology has improved over time from the grainy black-and-white photographs of the 1800s to the **high-definition** color images of today.

Camera obscura

Photography was invented in the early 1800s using a device called a camera obscura, which is Latin for dark room. The camera obscura projected an image onto a screen by letting light into a dark box through a small hole. Photographs were created by coating the screen with chemicals that react when exposed to light and record an image.

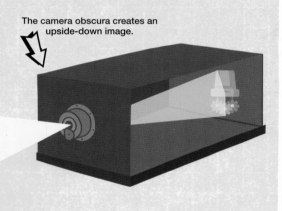

The camera obscura creates an upside-down image.

Nicéphore Niépce (1765–1833)

The oldest surviving photograph was taken by French inventor Niépce in 1826. He captured an image of the view from his window (see right). Niépce had to expose the screen to the light for several hours to create the image. This meant it was possible to capture only objects that were still.

Portrait photography

By the mid-1800s, photographic technology had improved, and new chemicals made it possible to capture an image with much shorter exposure times. This allowed photographers to take photos of people without them having to sit still for hours. British photographer Julia Margaret Cameron (1815–1879) was a pioneer in portrait photography, producing images with a high level of detail.

In 1864, Cameron took this photo of a young girl named Annie.

Thermal imaging

Light is a type of **electromagnetic radiation**. Our eyes see only visible light, but some cameras can detect other forms of radiation. Warm objects, such as bodies, give off **infrared** radiation, which is invisible to our eyes. Night-vision cameras sense infrared and turn it into images that we can see in the darkness of night. This is called thermal imaging.

Engineers use thermal imaging to check to see that machines are working correctly. The different colors represent different temperatures.

Going digital

A modern digital camera projects an image onto a light detector, which turns the image into electrical signals. The image can then be stored on the camera's memory.

PROJECT: INVISIBLE BEAMS

Remote controls for televisions or other equipment work by sending beams of radiation. We cannot see these beams, but the digital cameras on cell phones can pick them up.

You will need: a TV remote control and a cell phone

Place a remote control in front of the phone's camera and press some buttons on the remote control.

Do you see light flashing on the image on the phone's screen? The flashes you are seeing are infrared beams.

SENDING A MESSAGE

Before the discovery of electricity at the end of the 1700s, it took days to send a message from one part of a country to another. To reach a different part of the world, it could take weeks. The invention of the electronic telegraph allowed messages, called telegrams, to be sent almost instantly.

Samuel Morse
(1791–1872)

By the 1830s, many inventors around the world were experimenting with ways to send electrical signals along a wire. American inventor Samuel Morse created one of the first commercially useful telegraph systems. His system sent pulses of electricity along a single wire. Morse sent his first message over 3 miles (5 km) of wire in 1838.

Morse code

Telegraph systems transmit messages as a series of pulses. Samuel Morse created a code for his telegraph system that is still in use today. Morse code uses a combination of short pulses, or dots, and long pulses, or dashes, to represent letters and numbers.

A ●▬
B ▬●●●
C ▬●▬●
D ▬●●
E ●
F ●●▬●
G ▬▬●
H ●●●●
I ●●
J ●▬▬▬
K ▬●▬
L ●▬●●
M ▬▬
N ▬●
O ▬▬▬
P ●▬▬●
Q ▬▬●▬
R ●▬●

S ●●●
T ▬
U ●●▬
V ●●●▬
W ●▬▬
X ▬●●▬
Y ▬●▬▬
Z ▬▬●●
0 ▬▬▬▬▬
1 ●▬▬▬▬
2 ●●▬▬▬
3 ●●●▬▬
4 ●●●●▬
5 ●●●●●
6 ▬●●●●
7 ▬▬●●●
8 ▬▬▬●●
9 ▬▬▬▬●

Worldwide network

In the 1850s, telegraph wires were laid across the Atlantic Ocean in undersea cables, connecting Europe and North America. In 1902, a line across the Pacific Ocean finally encircled the world. Nearly instant worldwide communication was then possible.

Telegraph operators were highly skilled in sending and receiving coded messages.

International distress signal

Since 1908, SOS has been the standard international distress signal in Morse code. The message is a continuous sequence of three dots followed by three dashes, and was chosen because it is easy to recognize, even by people who are not trained in Morse code.

pROJeCT: TELEGRAPH SET

With the help of an adult, you can make your own telegraph set.

You will need: a 9V battery, three wooden boards, copper wire, insulated (wrapped in a casing) electric wire, a thin copper plate, a thin steel plate, a galvanized nail, screws, and a screwdriver

1. To make the transmitter, or sender, put a screw into one end of a board. Bend the copper strip slightly and position it over the screw, as shown. Screw the other end onto the board underneath the copper.

2. Create the electromagnetic receiver by wrapping copper wire around a nail. Hammer the nail into a board, and attach another board at a right angle to it. Attach the steel strip to it and hang it over the nail, as shown.

3. Use the electric wires to connect the transmitter and receiver to the battery, as shown.

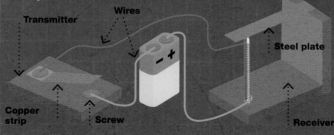

Transmitter
Wires
Steel plate
Copper strip
Screw
Receiver

When you press down on the copper plate to make it touch the screw on the transmitter, you should hear a click sound on the receiver. What happened?

LIGHTING OUR HOMES

The first electric lightbulb was made by English inventor Humphrey Davy in 1802. He sent an electrical current through a piece of **carbon**, making it glow brightly. However, Davy's bulb broke quickly and was far too bright to light a home. The first practical lightbulb was made more than 70 years later by American inventor Thomas Edison.

Thomas Edison (1847–1931)

Edison's lightbulb worked in a similar way to Davy's. It made a thin, thread-like **filament** glow by passing electricity through it. This is called an incandescent lightbulb. After experimenting with many different materials, Edison discovered that a filament made from carbonized bamboo would last for hundreds of hours before breaking. He set to work mass-producing his lightbulb.

Incandescent lightbulb ➡

🧠 How does it work?

An electric current runs between the support wire and the contact wire through the filament. This movement of electricity through the filament causes it to heat up and create light.

Coiled filament

Support wire

Contact wire

Connection to electricity

Saving energy

More than 90 percent of the energy needed to power an incandescent lightbulb is used to produce heat rather than light. In recent years, these bulbs have been replaced by more efficient bulbs.

Fluorescent lightbulbs produce light by passing an electric current through a gas. LED bulbs produce light by passing a current through a material called a semiconductor.

Fluorescent lightbulbs are many times more efficient than incandescent bulbs.

LED lightbulbs are even more efficient than fluorescent lightbulbs.

pROJeCT: MAKE A LIGHTBULB

You will need: Adult supervision, a large canning jar with a lid, a 9-volt battery, 3 feet (1 m) of insulated (wrapped in casing) copper wire, thin iron wire (such as unraveled picture-hanging wire)

Battery

Copper wire

Iron wire

1. Ask an adult to cut the copper wire in half and strip about 1 inch (2.5 cm) of the insulation off the ends of each piece. Ask an adult to punch two holes in the jar lid with a nail. Thread one end of each copper wire through the holes.

2. Make a hook on each end of the copper wire that will be inside the jar. Twist three strands of the iron wire together, then twist the ends around the hooks in the copper wire. This will be your filament.

3. Place the lid on the jar and carefully connect the free ends of the copper wire to each terminal on the battery. After connecting the battery, be careful not to touch the iron wire as it will get very hot.

What color light does your bulb give off?

TALKING ON THE LINE

Telephone receiver

While the telegraph could send messages a long distance, it could only transmit simple signals such as Morse code. In the 1870s, many inventors across the world were working on a way to transmit human voices across wires.

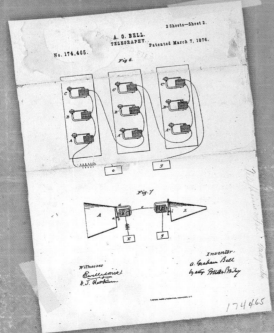

Alexander Graham Bell (1847–1922)

Although many others claimed to have invented the telephone before him, Scottish-born Alexander Graham Bell was the first to make a practical version. Working in Boston, Massachusetts, Bell found a way to turn the vibrations produced by the human voice into a changing electric current, which could then be carried over a telegraph line.

 Bell submitted this drawing of his telephone to the US **Patent** Office in 1876. The patent prevented others from using his invention without his permission. It caused a bitter disagreement with rival inventor Elisha Gray, who accused Bell of stealing his idea.

How it works

A telephone converts sound into electricity, then back into sound. A thin, vibrating sheet, called a diaphragm, in the mouthpiece of the telephone converts sound energy into an electrical current. The current travels along a line to the earpiece of the receiver. A diaphragm in the earpiece turns the electrical energy back into sound energy.

Making a connection

When you make a telephone call on a landline, or non-wireless line, the number you dial tells the switchboard which line you wish to connect to. The switchboard temporarily connects you to the number you are calling. The first telephone switchboards were operated by people. When someone wanted to make a call, he or she phoned an operator and told them the number they wished to be connected to. The operator would move the lines by plugging them into different sockets on a wooden board. Today, switchboards are operated by computer.

Switchboard

Mouthpiece

PROJECT: MAKE A STRING TELEPHONE

See how sounds can be transmitted as vibrations across a string.

You will need: Two large paper or disposable plastic cups, two paper clips, a 33-foot (10 m) piece of cotton string or fishing line, a friend, and a quiet area

1. Ask an adult to use a nail to punch a small hole in the center of the bottom of both cups. Thread the ends of the string up through the holes at the bottom of each cup.

2. Place a paperclip inside each cup and tie the string around it. (This is just to hold the string in place.)

3. Give one cup to your friend and walk slowly apart until the string is tight.

4. Hold the cup over your ear and ask your friend to talk into their cup, then reverse roles.

Can you hear your friend clearly? Try again, but let the string go loose. Next, try having a third person stand in the middle, holding the string. What happens?

AIRWAVE BROADCASTING

Radios work by receiving messages in the form of radio waves. The waves carry information that the radio turns into sound or pictures (see pages 20–21).

Guglielmo Marconi
(1874–1937)

Italian inventor Guglielmo Marconi developed a wireless version of the telegraph. It sent messages in Morse code (see pages 10—11) by radio waves. Due to a lack of interest in Italy, Marconi took his idea to Britain, where he found eager investors. The first wireless telegraph was sent in 1898 from France across the English Channel to Britain. Two years later, Marconi successfully sent a radio signal across the Atlantic Ocean. Soon large ships were equipped with radios. One of the first radio messages at sea was a call for help to aid the sinking ship *Titanic*, in 1912.

Sound broadcasting

In 1900, Brazilian priest Roberto Landell was the first person to broadcast a human voice by radio. Twenty years later, a radio station in Buenos Aires, Argentina, broadcast a live opera performance. At the time, only 20 homes in the city had receivers capable of picking up the broadcast. Just a few years later, radio had become a true means of mass communication.

Radio transmitters encode sound waves into a varying, or changing, electrical current. The current passes through an antenna, making electrons vibrate. This vibration produces radio waves.

The radio waves in turn make electrons in the receiver's antenna vibrate. This produces an electric current with the same pattern as the transmitter's current. The receiver decodes the pattern to turn the electrical current into sound.

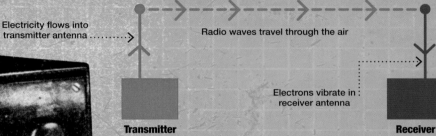

Electricity flows into transmitter antenna .... >

Radio waves travel through the air

Electrons vibrate in receiver antenna

Transmitter

Receiver

By 1915, Marconi was manufacturing powerful radio receivers for wireless telegraph stations. The Type 106 pictured here could pick up Morse code messages that had been transmitted thousands of miles away.

pROJeCT:
MAKE A METAL DETECTOR

See how radio waves can be used to detect metal.

You will need: an old battery-powered portable radio with AM and FM bands, a small battery-powered calculator (not solar-powered), batteries for both devices, and duct tape

1. Put the batteries in both devices. Switch the radio to AM and turn the dial far to the right so you only hear **static**. Turn the volume up high.

2. Turn on the calculator and hold it to the radio so the battery compartments are touching. Holding the two together, place them close to a metal object. If they are aligned correctly, you will hear a change in the static to a beeping sound. If you don't hear the beeps, adjust the position of the calculator until you do. Tape the radio and calculator together in this position.

3. Test out your metal detector on other objects.

How do you think this works?

MOTION PICTURES

Motion pictures, or movies, create the illusion of a moving image from a series of still images, called frames.

Eadweard Muybridge
(1830–1904)

In the 1870s, English photographer Eadweard Muybridge produced some of the earliest motion pictures. Muybridge set up a series of 12 cameras to photograph a horse in a sequence of shots. He put them together to create a moving image. One short movie played the first eleven frames below one after the other, revealing for the first time how a horse's legs move when it gallops.

Optical illusion

Movie projectors work by showing 24 different and separate frames per second. The feeling of movement is really just an **optical illusion**. The rapidly changing images fool our brains into thinking that we are seeing motion.

For early movies, film containing the sequence of frames was wound onto a reel. The reel was attached to a machine called a projector, and the film was fed into it. Newer movies are made using **digital** cameras, and the frames are saved onto a computer.

Panic station

Early filmgoers were not used to watching motion pictures, like the film *Train Pulling into a Station*, at left, by Auguste and Louis Lumière. Stories say that when it was first shown in Paris in 1896, audiences were scared by the image of a life-sized train moving toward them, and they tried to run away.

High definition

Some new movies are filmed using high-speed cameras that take 60 frames per second. This creates movies with greater detail and smoother movement. Many moviegoers complain that these films look too realistic. It seems that many of us like knowing that we're watching a movie, and that it isn't real.

PROJECT: FLIPBOOK ANIMATION

Make your own movie on a flipbook

You will need: a sticky notepad and a marker

1. Starting with the last sheet on the pad, draw a small dot in the bottom right-hand corner.

2. On the next sheet up, draw another dot a little to the left of the first dot. You can also make the dot slightly larger.

3. Repeat through the notepad, changing the position and size of the dot. Plot your own pattern around the pad.

4. To watch your movie, start from the back and use your thumb to flip through the pages of the book very quickly.

What do you see?

TURNING ON THE TV

Television was developed in the 1920s as a way to turn radio waves into a moving image on a screen.

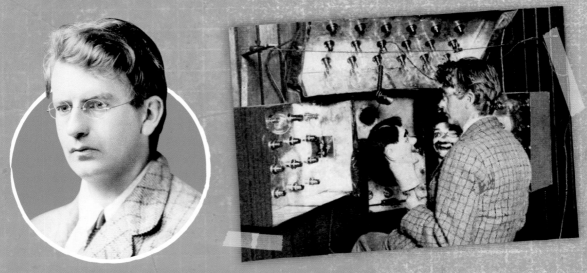

John Logie Baird (1888–1946)

The Scottish inventor John Logie Baird built the first practical TV in 1926. He demonstrated his invention by transmitting the image of a ventriloquist's dummy named Stooky Bill (above).

Mechanical TV

In the late 1920s, some radio stations began transmitting experimental TV signals. The signals were turned into images by a machine called a televisor, invented by John Logie Baird. A spinning metal disk with a series of holes in it passed in front of a **neon** lamp. Each hole represented one line on the image. The radio signal changed the brightness of the lamp at each point. This created a dim orange image about 1.5 inches (4 cm) square.

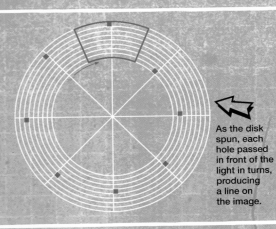

As the disk spun, each hole passed in front of the light in turns, producing a line on the image.

Electronic TV

In the 1930s, electronic TVs replaced Baird's mechanical TV, and the first commercial television stations began broadcasting. Electronic televisions created an image by firing a beam of electrons at a fluorescent screen. The beam scanned across the screen, changing its energy to create different levels of brightness at each point. Today, newer televisions use a digital signal to create an image on the screen.

Magnetic plates send the electrons to different points on the screen

Path of electrons

Bright spot

Heated filament gives off a stream of electrons

The electrons are focused and sped up

Fluorescent screen

PROJECT: RAINBOW SPINNER

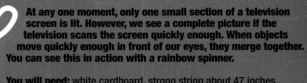

At any one moment, only one small section of a television screen is lit. However, we see a complete picture if the television scans the screen quickly enough. When objects move quickly enough in front of our eyes, they merge together. You can see this in action with a rainbow spinner.

You will need: white cardboard, strong string about 47 inches (120 cm) long, colored pencils or crayons, a sharp pencil, and scissors

1. Cut out a cardboard disk and divide it into seven equal segments. Color the segments with the seven colors of the rainbow, as shown.

2. Make two holes with the pencil near the center of the disk about 0.5 inches (1.25 cm) apart. Thread the string through the holes, making a loop at each end. Put a finger through the end of each loop and flip the disk over the string several times until the string is well twisted. Now pull your hands apart to tighten the string, then let the string go loose. Repeat these actions and the disk should spin.

What do you see when the disk spins?

SENDING SAFE SIGNALS

Whenever we send a message through technology, there is always the chance a stranger may be able to see, hear, or read it. Creating secret codes to keep messages safe is called encryption. Various methods have been created to encrypt messages, and today encryption is an important part of the Internet.

Hedy Lamarr (1914–2000)

Better known as a film star, Hedy Lamarr was also an ingenious inventor. During World War II, she invented a code to protect radio signals sent to **torpedoes**. The frequency, or number of repetitions, of radio signals was varied using the same device used in a **player piano**. An enemy could not block the signal without knowing the code. Because the frequency was constantly being changed, the code was, too. Lamarr's invention is now used in Bluetooth and wireless, or Wi-Fi, technology.

Code breakers

During World War II, the German Navy developed the Enigma machine to encrypt its messages. The Germans believed that their code was unbreakable. But a team of British cryptographers, or people who make and break codes, finally managed to break Enigma's code using their own machine, called the Bombe. Their work remained a secret for many years afterward.

The Enigma machine used a series of rotating disks to code messages.

Public key encryption

A common method of encryption is called public key encryption. Here's how it works:

1. Ally wants to send an expensive diamond to Jane but doesn't want it stolen on the way.

2. Jane sends Ally an unlocked padlock, for which only Jane has the key.

3. Ally puts the diamond in a box and locks it with the padlock.

4. On receiving the box, Jane removes the padlock with the key.

Encryption on the Internet works in a similar way. Jane sends out a public key to Ally to use to encrypt her messages in digital code. When Ally sends Jane an encrypted message, Jane uses a private key to decode the message. The private key allows Jane to see and retrieve all messages to her, but Ally's public key only allows her to see what she herself put in there for Jane.

Caesar cipher

Codes have been used to keep secrets for thousands of years. More than 2,000 years ago, Roman general Julius Caesar used a code called a substitution **cipher**. He substituted one letter for the letter that appeared a fixed number of positions away from it in the alphabet. He wrapped the alphabet around, so that Z came before A. In the example below, each letter is substituted with the letter that appears three spaces before it in the alphabet. For example, E becomes B.

A	B	C	D	E	F	G	A	I
X	Y	Z	A	B	C	D	E	F

PROJECT: SECRET MESSAGES

When making your own secret messages, it helps to write out the alphabet.

You will need: a pen, paper, and some friends

One way to do this is to write the alphabet in 13 rows of two letters, with AB at the top. Substitute the letters in a message with the code (–2), which means change each letter to the letter directly above it. To substitute for (+4), change each letter to the letter two rows below. Create your own encrypted messages and see if your friends can decipher them.

O D O V I N   J A   O Z X C I J G J B T

Cracking codes gets easier with practice. Can you crack this Caesar cipher? What cipher has been used?

THE WORLD WIDE WEB

By the mid 1980s, computers across the world were linked to one another in a network called the Internet. But there was no easy way to find the information stored on other computers. The World Wide Web allowed computer users to create websites full of information with addresses that other users could search for. Invented in 1989, it marked the start of an information explosion.

Tim Berners-Lee
(1955–)

The World Wide Web was invented by the British physicist Tim Berners-Lee. He created the first website in 1991 for the physics research institute CERN, where he was working at the time. The website told visitors how to search the Web and create their own websites. Berners-Lee has campaigned ever since to promote open access for everyone to information on the Web.

Internet explosion

Today, four billion people use the Internet. That's more than half the world's population. China has the most people accessing the Internet, at 800 million users. There are more than 1.9 billion websites on the Web, and more than 5 billion pages. To print out the entire Web, you would need more than 100 billion sheets of paper.

PROJECT: SEARCH THE WEB

There is an enormous amount of information on the Internet, but not all of it is reliable. Here are a few tips for using search engines.

You will need: a computer with Internet connection

WWW.

1. Search engines find results by scouring the Internet for keywords input by you, the user. The keywords are related to what is being searched for. Putting "quotation marks" around keywords helps find an exact match of those words.

2. Once you have done a search, a list of results will show you links to sites related to your keywords. The strongest matches will be near the top. However, it is worth scrolling down the page because some websites pay extra to come out at the top of a search, whether they match the keywords closely or not.

3. When you select a website, you need to decide if you can trust the information. Domain names, or Web addresses, that end in .edu or .gov are educational and government websites that are normally reliable. Also look for official organizations, such as NASA, who put a lot of useful information on the Web.

4. Always be critical of what you read. Doublecheck anything you're not sure of by looking for matching information on a trusted website.

Compare search results on different search engines, such as Google, Bing, or Yahoo. Which ones do you think work best?

Google is the world's most visited search engine. More than 5 billion searches are made on Google every day.

CELL PHONE REVOLUTION

Cell phones allow us to send and receive calls while on the move. Today, more than four billion people own a cell phone, and many of us never leave home without one.

John Francis Mitchell (1928–2009)

The idea of a cell phone **network** was first developed by John Mitchell, the chief engineer of the Motorola phone company. The first **prototype** was made in 1973, and cell phones went on sale to the public ten years later. The first cell phone available for sale to the public, the DynaTAC 8000X, was 13 inches (33 cm) long, weighed nearly 1.7 pounds (784 g), and cost $4,000. It was nicknamed "the Brick."

The first cell phones were large and heavy. These were replaced in the 1990s by much smaller and lighter models.

Today, many cell phones have become larger again to give them a bigger screen. Modern smartphones are small, portable computers.

How does a cell phone call work?

Cell phones can only send signals over short distances. To make a call, you need to send a signal to a nearby cell-phone tower. The call is relayed to the cell-phone tower nearest to the person you are calling, which then sends the signal to their phone. To stay in touch, the network needs to know where you are, so your phone sends out a signal as soon as you turn it on.

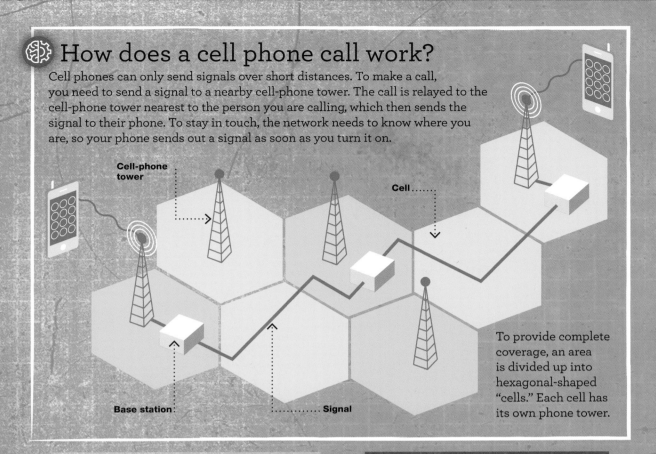

Cell-phone tower

Cell

Base station

Signal

To provide complete coverage, an area is divided up into hexagonal-shaped "cells." Each cell has its own phone tower.

Satellite phones

You cannot send or receive a call on a cell phone if you are outside the boundaries of a cell network. **Satellite** phones work in a similar way to cell phones, but they send a signal to a satellite in orbit around Earth instead of to a phone tower. The phones have large antennas to produce a powerful signal. Unlike cell phones, they can send and receive messages from almost anywhere on the planet, and are often carried by people traveling to remote areas.

Satellite phones send messages through a network of satellites in orbit 500 miles (800 km) above Earth.

pROJECT: NO DISTRACTIONS

People should never use cell phones while they are driving because it takes their eyes off the road. Test how distracting cell phones can be with this experiment.

You will need: a yardstick (meter stick), test subjects, and a stopwatch

1. To test your subject's reactions, hold the stick at the top mark and ask the subject to place his or her thumb and forefinger surrounding the 0 mark without touching the stick. Ask them to catch the stick when you let go of it, and then record the distance it falls. This is a measure of the subject's reaction time. Perform several trials to produce an average score.

2. Repeat the test while the subject is talking on a cell phone.

3. Repeat the test while the subject is texting.

Does using a cell phone slow reaction times? Which is more distracting—talking or texting?

FINDING OUR WAY

Today, the Global Positioning System (GPS) has largely replaced maps as the method we use to find our way to a destination. Typing an address into the satellite **navigation** system, or satnav, beams radio signals up to satellites in orbit around the planet, and back down to us.

Roger Easton (1921–2014)

American physicist Roger Easton came up with the idea of a satellite navigation system while working for the US Navy in the 1960s. He called his system Time-Navigation, because it relied on the use of highly accurate clocks. Renamed GPS, it was launched in 1973, initially just for use by the US military. It was made available for public use in the 1980s.

The network of GPS satellites provides coverage for almost the entire planet. Each satellite carries a clock that is accurate to within one billionth of a second.

Satellite system

There are currently 31 GPS satellites in orbit 12,550 miles (20,200 km) above Earth. A satnav's signal must reach at least four satellites for GPS to find its location. It does this by measuring the time it takes the signal to reach each satellite. This gives the distance from each satellite. GPS calculates the location from these four distances, using a process called triangulation.

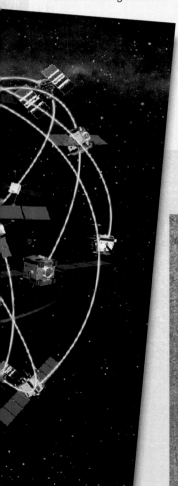

Triangulation

As its name suggests, triangulation works by creating triangles. In two dimensions, the calculation is simpler. Imagine a hiker trying to reach a friend who is transmitting a signal to him. He does not know how far he will have to walk.

1. He can tell what direction the radio waves are coming from, but not how far away they are.

2. He draws a line from himself toward the direction of the signal.

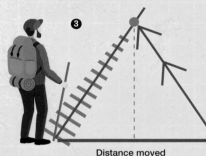

Distance moved

3. He then walks to another location and takes a second reading, drawing a line in the new direction of the signal. His friend is at the place where the two lines meet. He can use math called **trigonometry** to figure out how far away that is.

PROJECT: HUMAN SATNAV

Satnavs need to give accurate instructions to drivers to make sure they stay on track. Act as a human satnav and guide a friend from one part of your school to another.

You will need: a pen, some paper, and your school

1. First you need to record your route. Choose a starting point in your school and an endpoint at a distant part of the school. Walk the entire route from your starting point, writing down each step of your journey. Arrange your instructions as clearly as you can.

2. Start by recording the direction you are facing as you begin your journey. Count the number of steps you take before making your first turn. Describe the angle of the turn and any doors you need to open, then proceed to your next turn. Continue until you reach your destination. At each stage, record how many steps your friend will need to take before the next turn.

3. Now hand your instructions over to your friend and take them to the starting point.

Did they make it to their destination without getting lost?

GLOSSARY

CARBON A chemical element found in all living plants and animals

CIPHER A method of turning a message into a secret code

CIRCUIT A pathway for electricity to flow without interruption

DIGITAL Describes something relating to electronic or computerized technology

ELECTROMAGNETIC RADIATION A form of energy that is transmitted in waves, such as light

ELECTRONS Tiny particles that form part of the atoms of matter. Electrons have a negative electric charge and flow to produce electricity.

ENGINEER Someone who designs and builds machinery or technical equipment

FILAMENT A thread-like wire inside a lightbulb that glows when an electric current is passed through it

FLUORESCENT A property of a substance that means it glows when electricity or other waves of energy flow through it

HIGH-DEFINITION Television or computer screens that display a high level of detail in their images

INFRARED A form of electromagnetic radiation with a slightly longer wavelength than visible light. Warm objects radiate infrared.

LED Short for Light-Emitting Diode, a device that gives off light of one particular color when electricity is passed through it

MACHINE A piece of equipment used to do a certain kind of work

NAVIGATION A system used to plan how to get from one place to another

NEON A gas that can be used to make brightly glowing colored lights

NETWORK A system of computers or devices that are connected to each other

OPTICAL ILLUSION The use of light, color, and pattern to trick the brain into seeing something that is not real

PATENT A license that gives an inventor sole right to make, use, or sell their invention for a period of time

PLAYER PIANO A self-playing piano that is programmed to play using a roll of perforated paper

PROTOTYPE A model that is made to test a new invention or design

ROBOTIC Describes a type of machine that is programmed to perform tasks

STATIC A crackling noise made by radios or televisions, caused by atmospheric interference

TORPEDOES Underwater missiles that launch from ships or submarines and travel under their own power toward their targets

TRIGONOMETRY A branch of mathematics that deals with the properties of triangles

ANSWERS

p. 7 Ice cube tray battery

The more cells you add to your battery, the stronger the electric current, so the LED will shine brighter.

p. 11 Telegraph set

When you touch the copper plate to the screw, you complete an electric circuit. This powers the electromagnet, which pulls the strip above it down to make a click. When you break the circuit, the electromagnet loses its magnetism.

p. 13 Make a lightbulb

The iron filament resists the electrical flow and heats up. It should give off a bright red light before burning out. Do not to touch it right away afterward. It will still be very hot.

p. 15 Make a string telephone

Your voice vibrates the air inside the cup. The vibrations are transferred to the string and make the air inside your friend's cup vibrate, and they should hear your voice clearly. If the string is slack or being held, the vibrations do not transfer across the string.

p. 17 Make a metal detector

The circuit board of the calculator gives off weak radio waves. Those waves bounce off metal objects and the radio picks them up and amplifies them.

p. 19 Flipbook animation

If you flip the book quickly enough, the dot will appear to move around and grow larger and smaller.

p. 23 Secret messages

TITANS OF TECHNOLOGY
The cipher in this case is -5.

p. 21 Rainbow spinner

When you spin the disk, the colors merge together to make the spinner look white. We see all the colors all over the disk at the same time, and when mixed together, the colors of the rainbow make a white light.

p. 27 Cell phones

The distracted subjects should have longer reaction times. Texting is usually more distracting than talking.

INDEX

SPIRITUAL SELF CARE FOR BLACK WOMEN

A JOURNEY TO SELF DISCOVERY: 12 MONTH PLANNER & GUIDED JOURNAL WITH SELF REFLECTION ACTIVITIES

stress less
PRESS | stresslesspress.com

CHECK OUT OUR OTHER SELF CARE BOOKS

SELF CARE WORKBOOK FOR BLACK WOMEN

A 160+ page activity book covering mental, physical, spiritual and emotional self help practices. Complete with a 12-month planner and guided journal

EMOTIONAL SELF CARE FOR BLACK WOMEN

A self help activity book to address the thoughts, beliefs and triggers which affect your emotions and behavior

THE MENTAL HEALTH MIXTAPE FOR BLACK MEN

A workbook to help Black men develop coping skills and self care strategies to keep their mental health on track

Stress Less Press are a Black-owned independent publisher.
If you enjoy this book, please consider supporting us by leaving a review on Amazon!

INTRODUCTION

The beauty of spiritual self care is it can mean different things to different people. For some it's about connecting with a higher power through prayer or worship, but for others it can mean being in nature or giving back to their community.

A common misconception is that spiritual self care is only for religious folk, but this couldn't be further from the truth! Anyone can practice spiritual self care, as it is simply the act of taking care of the soul - which of course is subjective.

Due to the societal challenges we face, spiritual self care is not always a priority for Black women as we manage the complexities of caring for others whilst navigating the intersections of race and gender. However, it's *because* of the roles and responsibilities we adopt in our personal and professional lives that make spiritual self care is such a necessary support tool. Black women deserve the time and space to seek a life of meaning and purpose.

When we practice spiritual self care, we tune into our 'inner self'; what our true purpose is, what our true values are and what our true desires are. The self care aspect comes in when we recognize who our inner self is, and honor this on a daily basis. If you're reading this and feeling unsure of who your inner self is, then this book is a great place to start on your journey of self discovery.

Continued repetition of positive habits are what make for long-term spiritual wellness. The best way to do this is to implement small self care habits every day. Use the 52 week planner to schedule a little bit of love and attention for your soul.

In this book you'll find a range of spiritual self discovery activities to get you started on your journey, followed by 52 weeks of planner space to schedule your spiritual self care activities and more. Alongside this are guided journal pages to check in with yourself, reflect and unload your feelings.

Please note that the spiritual self care activities in this book are not a substitute for the help offered by mental health professionals. If you are struggling to cope, please consult your GP. You can also find a list of resources at the back of the book.

SELF CARE ASSESSMENT

Fill in this form to assess how often you've engaged in spiritual self care activities over the past 2 weeks. Activities that you've found yourself practicing 'never' or 'rarely' are an indication of areas you might want to prioritize on your spiritual self care journey

1 = Never   2 = Rarely   3 = Sometimes   4 = Often

	1	2	3	4
I practiced prayer or meditation	○	○	○	○
I took time for personal reflection (e.g. journalling)	○	○	○	○
I spent time in nature	○	○	○	○
I engaged in non-work / school related hobbies	○	○	○	○
I connected with others	○	○	○	○
I made time to read / listen to things that inspire me	○	○	○	○
I focused on being present in the here-and-now	○	○	○	○
I expressed my creativity (e.g. art, cooking, dancing)	○	○	○	○
I have practiced gratitude	○	○	○	○

 While you ideally want to be practising each self care behavior often, but don't worry if you aren't. Remember to be kind to yourself. You're a work in progress!

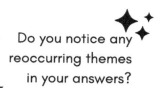

Do you notice any
reoccurring themes
in your answers?

SELF DISCOVERY QUESTIONNAIRE

Asking self discovery questions is the best way to gain clarity on your life's path and apply creative solutions to get you where you want to be

What values are important to you?

What does your dream life look like?

Who do you admire and why?

Which three words describe you best?

What makes you feel motived, inspired or excited?

What would you do with your life if you had a guarantee of success?

DATE

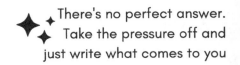
There's no perfect answer.
Take the pressure off and
just write what comes to you

YOUR LIFE PURPOSE

'Finding your purpose' is more than just a cliché or a dream that's
out of reach. Trying to understand the below elements can help
lead you to a better, happier life

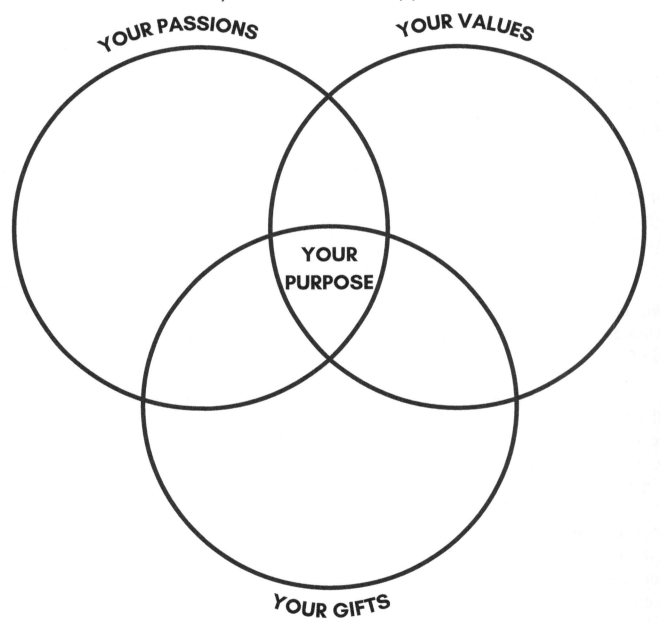

YOUR PASSIONS

YOUR VALUES

YOUR
PURPOSE

YOUR GIFTS

Have you
decided your
purpose? Write
it here

When and how will you start
the journey to being
unapologetically you?

BE YOU, FOR YOU
SELF PORTRAIT

For Black women, showing up as our authentic selves can be challenging when we live in a world that doesn't always accept us. As hard as it is, being true to yourself can do so much for self esteem and mental health. Use words/drawings to reflect on the person you show to the world versus who you truly are

THE INNER ME   **THE OUTER ME**

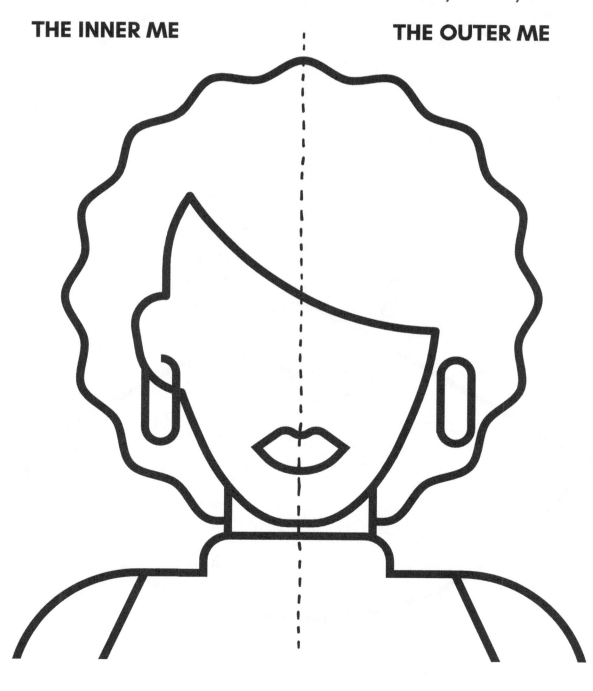

DATE

LIFE BALANCE CHART

Balance is essential to achieving spiritual self care. Often when
we feel stressed or unfulfilled, it's because our balance is off.
Fill in the pie chart below detailing what activities you do (or plan
to do) for connection, achievement and enjoyment

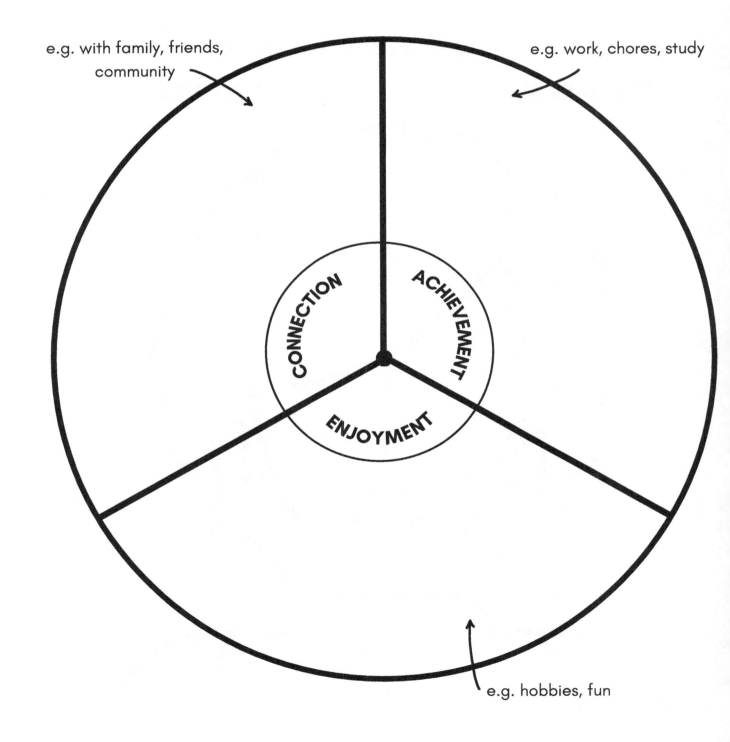

e.g. with family, friends,
community

e.g. work, chores, study

CONNECTION

ACHIEVEMENT

ENJOYMENT

e.g. hobbies, fun

Cut out your drawing and
display it somewhere that
you will see it every day!

AFFIRMATION DRAWING

Think of an affirmation, e.g. "I am beautiful and worthy of love"
and use the space below to draw or write what this means to
you. (Don't worry if you're not a natural when it comes to drawing,
focus on how it feels to be creative and expressive)

SPIRITUAL SELF CARE IDEAS

Below you'll find a non-exhaustive list of spiritual self care practices that you can easily implement over the next 52 weeks as you build a self care routine

- [ ] Meditation
- [ ] Spend time alone
- [ ] Coloring or doodling
- [ ] Journalling
- [ ] Yoga
- [ ] Go on a nature walk
- [ ] Social media detox
- [ ] Volunteer in your community
- [ ] Quality time with your favorite person
- [ ] Clean your space
- [ ] Write a gratitude list
- [ ] Gardening
- [ ] Create a vision board
- [ ] Goof around and have fun!

SPIRITUAL SELF CARE IDEAS

Spiritual self care is subjective, and you know yourself best.
Use the space below to jot down any ideas you have for activities
to feed your soul

- [ ]
- [ ]
- [ ]
- [ ]
- [ ]
- [ ]
- [ ]
- [ ]
- [ ]
- [ ]
- [ ]
- [ ]
- [ ]

W/C

_____

SELF CARE PLANNER

Carving out time for yourself everyday is the key to sustained spiritual self care. What will you do for <u>you</u> this week?

MON _____

TUES _____

WEDS _____

THURS _____

FRI _____

SAT _____

SUN _____

MY GOALS FOR THE WEEK

_____ ☐

_____ ☐

_____ ☐

_____ ☐

_____ ☐

MY AFFIRMATION FOR THE WEEK

WHAT I DID WELL THIS WEEK

WHAT I'D LIKE TO WORK ON NEXT WEEK

WEEKLY JOURNAL

Don't overthink it. Just write
If you're struggling, here's a prompt to get you started:
What's stopping you from being happier?

_____
_____
_____
_____
_____
_____
_____
_____
_____
_____
_____
_____
_____
_____
_____
_____
_____
_____
_____
_____
_____
_____
_____
_____
_____
_____

W/C

Aim for a balance of
<u>achievement</u>, <u>connection</u>
and <u>enjoyment</u> in your week!

SELF CARE PLANNER

Carving out time for yourself everyday is the key to sustained
spiritual self care. What will you do for <u>you</u> this week?

MON _____

TUES _____

WEDS _____

THURS _____

FRI _____

SAT _____

SUN _____

MY GOALS
FOR THE WEEK

_____ ☐

_____ ☐

_____ ☐

_____ ☐

_____ ☐

MY AFFIRMATION
FOR THE WEEK

WHAT I DID WELL
THIS WEEK

WHAT I'D LIKE TO WORK
ON NEXT WEEK

W/C

WEEKLY JOURNAL

Don't overthink it. Just write
If you're struggling, here's a prompt to get you started:
Where does your self worth come from?

W/C

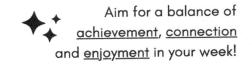
SELF CARE PLANNER

Carving out time for yourself everyday is the key to sustained spiritual self care. What will you do for <u>you</u> this week?

MON _____

TUES _____

WEDS _____

THURS _____

FRI _____

SAT _____

SUN _____

**MY GOALS
FOR THE WEEK**

**MY AFFIRMATION
FOR THE WEEK**

**WHAT I DID WELL
THIS WEEK**

**WHAT I'D LIKE TO WORK
ON NEXT WEEK**

WEEKLY JOURNAL

Don't overthink it. Just write
If you're struggling, here's a prompt to get you started:
When do you feel most alive and present in your life?

W/C

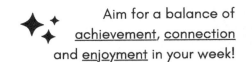

Aim for a balance of
<u>achievement</u>, <u>connection</u>
and <u>enjoyment</u> in your week!

SELF CARE PLANNER

Carving out time for yourself everyday is the key to sustained spiritual self care. What will you do for <u>you</u> this week?

MON _____

TUES _____

WEDS _____

THURS _____

FRI _____

SAT _____

SUN _____

MY GOALS
FOR THE WEEK

_____ ☐

_____ ☐

_____ ☐

_____ ☐

_____ ☐

MY AFFIRMATION
FOR THE WEEK

WHAT I DID WELL
THIS WEEK

WHAT I'D LIKE TO WORK
ON NEXT WEEK

WEEKLY JOURNAL

Don't overthink it. Just write
If you're struggling, here's a prompt to get you started:
What do you need that you aren't getting?

W/C

_____

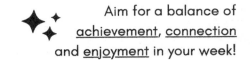

SELF CARE PLANNER

Carving out time for yourself everyday is the key to sustained spiritual self care. What will you do for <u>you</u> this week?

MON _____

TUES _____

WEDS _____

THURS _____

FRI _____

SAT _____

SUN _____

MY GOALS FOR THE WEEK

_____ ☐

_____ ☐

_____ ☐

_____ ☐

_____ ☐

MY AFFIRMATION FOR THE WEEK

WHAT I DID WELL THIS WEEK

WHAT I'D LIKE TO WORK ON NEXT WEEK

WEEKLY JOURNAL

Don't overthink it. Just write
If you're struggling, here's a prompt to get you started:
What is your definition of success?

_____
_____
_____
_____
_____
_____
_____
_____
_____
_____
_____
_____
_____
_____
_____
_____
_____
_____
_____
_____
_____
_____
_____
_____
_____
_____
_____

W/C

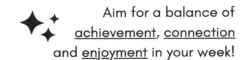

SELF CARE PLANNER

Carving out time for yourself everyday is the key to sustained spiritual self care. What will you do for <u>you</u> this week?

MON _____

TUES _____

WEDS _____

THURS _____

FRI _____

SAT _____

SUN _____

MY GOALS FOR THE WEEK

_____ ☐

_____ ☐

_____ ☐

_____ ☐

_____ ☐

MY AFFIRMATION FOR THE WEEK

WHAT I DID WELL THIS WEEK

WHAT I'D LIKE TO WORK ON NEXT WEEK

WEEKLY JOURNAL

Don't overthink it. Just write

If you're struggling, here's a prompt to get you started:

What are the things you're most grateful for?

W/C

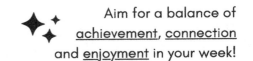
Aim for a balance of
achievement, connection
and enjoyment in your week!

SELF CARE PLANNER

Carving out time for yourself everyday is the key to sustained spiritual self care. What will you do for you this week?

MON _____

TUES _____

WEDS _____

THURS _____

FRI _____

SAT _____

SUN _____

MY GOALS
FOR THE WEEK

_____ ☐

_____ ☐

_____ ☐

_____ ☐

_____ ☐

MY AFFIRMATION
FOR THE WEEK

WHAT I DID WELL
THIS WEEK

WHAT I'D LIKE TO WORK
ON NEXT WEEK

WEEKLY JOURNAL

Don't overthink it. Just write

If you're struggling, here's a prompt to get you started:

Do you ever feel jealous or envious of others? If so, why?

W/C

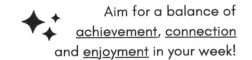

SELF CARE PLANNER

Carving out time for yourself everyday is the key to sustained spiritual self care. What will you do for <u>you</u> this week?

MON _____

TUES _____

WEDS _____

THURS _____

FRI _____

SAT _____

SUN _____

MY GOALS FOR THE WEEK

_____ ☐

_____ ☐

_____ ☐

_____ ☐

_____ ☐

MY AFFIRMATION FOR THE WEEK

WHAT I DID WELL THIS WEEK

WHAT I'D LIKE TO WORK ON NEXT WEEK

WEEKLY JOURNAL

Don't overthink it. Just write

If you're struggling, here's a prompt to get you started:

What are 5 personality traits that you're proud of

W/C
_____

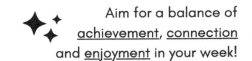
Aim for a balance of
<u>achievement</u>, <u>connection</u>
and <u>enjoyment</u> in your week!

SELF CARE PLANNER

Carving out time for yourself everyday is the key to sustained spiritual self care. What will you do for <u>you</u> this week?

MON   _____

TUES   _____

WEDS   _____

THURS   _____

FRI   _____

SAT   _____

SUN   _____

MY GOALS FOR THE WEEK

_____ ☐

_____ ☐

_____ ☐

_____ ☐

_____ ☐

MY AFFIRMATION FOR THE WEEK

WHAT I DID WELL THIS WEEK

WHAT I'D LIKE TO WORK ON NEXT WEEK

WEEKLY JOURNAL

Don't overthink it. Just write
If you're struggling, here's a prompt to get you started:
What's your favorite part of the day?

W/C
_____

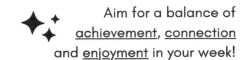

SELF CARE PLANNER

Carving out time for yourself everyday is the key to sustained spiritual self care. What will you do for <u>you</u> this week?

MON _____

TUES _____

WEDS _____

THURS _____

FRI _____

SAT _____

SUN _____

MY GOALS FOR THE WEEK

_____ ☐

_____ ☐

_____ ☐

_____ ☐

_____ ☐

MY AFFIRMATION FOR THE WEEK

WHAT I DID WELL THIS WEEK

WHAT I'D LIKE TO WORK ON NEXT WEEK

WEEKLY JOURNAL

Don't overthink it. Just write
If you're struggling, here's a prompt to get you started:
What can you do to achieve more peace in your life?

W/C
_____

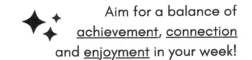

Aim for a balance of
<u>achievement</u>, <u>connection</u>
and <u>enjoyment</u> in your week!

SELF CARE PLANNER

Carving out time for yourself everyday is the key to sustained
spiritual self care. What will you do for <u>you</u> this week?

MON _____

TUES _____

WEDS _____

THURS _____

FRI _____

SAT _____

SUN _____

MY GOALS
FOR THE WEEK

_____ ☐

_____ ☐

_____ ☐

_____ ☐

_____ ☐

MY AFFIRMATION
FOR THE WEEK

WHAT I DID WELL
THIS WEEK

WHAT I'D LIKE TO WORK
ON NEXT WEEK

WEEKLY JOURNAL

Don't overthink it. Just write
If you're struggling, here's a prompt to get you started:
How would you like to be remembered?

W/C

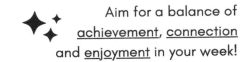

SELF CARE PLANNER

Carving out time for yourself everyday is the key to sustained spiritual self care. What will you do for <u>you</u> this week?

MON _____

TUES _____

WEDS _____

THURS _____

FRI _____

SAT _____

SUN _____

MY GOALS FOR THE WEEK

_____ ☐

_____ ☐

_____ ☐

_____ ☐

_____ ☐

MY AFFIRMATION FOR THE WEEK

WHAT I DID WELL THIS WEEK

WHAT I'D LIKE TO WORK ON NEXT WEEK

WEEKLY JOURNAL

Don't overthink it. Just write
If you're struggling, here's a prompt to get you started:
What's stopping you from being happier?

W / C

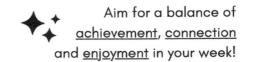

Aim for a balance of
<u>achievement</u>, <u>connection</u>
and <u>enjoyment</u> in your week!

SELF CARE PLANNER

Carving out time for yourself everyday is the key to sustained
spiritual self care. What will you do for <u>you</u> this week?

MON _____

TUES _____

WEDS _____

THURS _____

FRI _____

SAT _____

SUN _____

MY GOALS
FOR THE WEEK

_____ ☐

_____ ☐

_____ ☐

_____ ☐

_____ ☐

MY AFFIRMATION
FOR THE WEEK

WHAT I DID WELL
THIS WEEK

WHAT I'D LIKE TO WORK
ON NEXT WEEK

WEEKLY JOURNAL

Don't overthink it. Just write
If you're struggling, here's a prompt to get you started:
What inspires you the most?

W/C

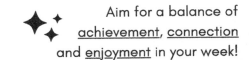

Aim for a balance of <u>achievement</u>, <u>connection</u> and <u>enjoyment</u> in your week!

SELF CARE PLANNER

Carving out time for yourself everyday is the key to sustained spiritual self care. What will you do for <u>you</u> this week?

MON _____

TUES _____

WEDS _____

THURS _____

FRI _____

SAT _____

SUN _____

MY GOALS FOR THE WEEK

_____ ☐

_____ ☐

_____ ☐

_____ ☐

_____ ☐

MY AFFIRMATION FOR THE WEEK

WHAT I DID WELL THIS WEEK

WHAT I'D LIKE TO WORK ON NEXT WEEK

WEEKLY JOURNAL

Don't overthink it. Just write
If you're struggling, here's a prompt to get you started:
Who brings you the most joy in your life?

W/C

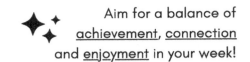

SELF CARE PLANNER

Carving out time for yourself everyday is the key to sustained spiritual self care. What will you do for <u>you</u> this week?

MON _____

TUES _____

WEDS _____

THURS _____

FRI _____

SAT _____

SUN _____

MY GOALS
FOR THE WEEK

_____ ☐

_____ ☐

_____ ☐

_____ ☐

_____ ☐

MY AFFIRMATION
FOR THE WEEK

WHAT I DID WELL
THIS WEEK

WHAT I'D LIKE TO WORK
ON NEXT WEEK

WEEKLY JOURNAL

Don't overthink it. Just write

If you're struggling, here's a prompt to get you started:

What actions do you take to stay connected to others?

_____

_____

_____

_____

_____

_____

_____

_____

_____

_____

_____

_____

_____

_____

_____

_____

_____

_____

_____

_____

_____

_____

_____

_____

_____

_____

W/C

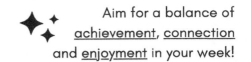

SELF CARE PLANNER

Carving out time for yourself everyday is the key to sustained spiritual self care. What will you do for <u>you</u> this week?

MON _____

TUES _____

WEDS _____

THURS _____

FRI _____

SAT _____

SUN _____

MY GOALS FOR THE WEEK

_____ ☐

_____ ☐

_____ ☐

_____ ☐

_____ ☐

MY AFFIRMATION FOR THE WEEK

WHAT I DID WELL THIS WEEK

WHAT I'D LIKE TO WORK ON NEXT WEEK

WEEKLY JOURNAL

Don't overthink it. Just write
If you're struggling, here's a prompt to get you started:
What would you tell your younger self?

W/C

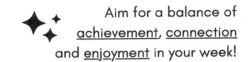

SELF CARE PLANNER

Carving out time for yourself everyday is the key to sustained spiritual self care. What will you do for <u>you</u> this week?

MON _____

TUES _____

WEDS _____

THURS _____

FRI _____

SAT _____

SUN _____

MY GOALS FOR THE WEEK

_____ ☐

_____ ☐

_____ ☐

_____ ☐

_____ ☐

MY AFFIRMATION FOR THE WEEK

WHAT I DID WELL THIS WEEK

WHAT I'D LIKE TO WORK ON NEXT WEEK

WEEKLY JOURNAL

Don't overthink it. Just write
If you're struggling, here's a prompt to get you started:
What is your biggest aspiration in life?

W/C _____

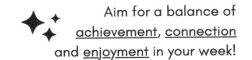

Aim for a balance of
<u>achievement</u>, <u>connection</u>
and <u>enjoyment</u> in your week!

SELF CARE PLANNER

Carving out time for yourself everyday is the key to sustained spiritual self care. What will you do for <u>you</u> this week?

MON _____

TUES _____

WEDS _____

THURS _____

FRI _____

SAT _____

SUN _____

MY GOALS FOR THE WEEK

_____ ☐

_____ ☐

_____ ☐

_____ ☐

_____ ☐

MY AFFIRMATION FOR THE WEEK

WHAT I DID WELL THIS WEEK

WHAT I'D LIKE TO WORK ON NEXT WEEK

WEEKLY JOURNAL

Don't overthink it. Just write

If you're struggling, here's a prompt to get you started:

What are the biggest life lessons your learned so far?

W/C

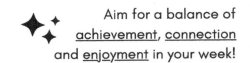
Aim for a balance of
<u>achievement</u>, <u>connection</u>
and <u>enjoyment</u> in your week!

SELF CARE PLANNER

Carving out time for yourself everyday is the key to sustained spiritual self care. What will you do for <u>you</u> this week?

MON _____

TUES _____

WEDS _____

THURS _____

FRI _____

SAT _____

SUN _____

MY GOALS FOR THE WEEK

_____ ☐

_____ ☐

_____ ☐

_____ ☐

_____ ☐

MY AFFIRMATION FOR THE WEEK

WHAT I DID WELL THIS WEEK

WHAT I'D LIKE TO WORK ON NEXT WEEK

WEEKLY JOURNAL

Don't overthink it. Just write
If you're struggling, here's a prompt to get you started:
Where do you see yourself in 5 years?

W/C

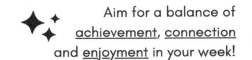

SELF CARE PLANNER

Carving out time for yourself everyday is the key to sustained spiritual self care. What will you do for <u>you</u> this week?

MON _____

TUES _____

WEDS _____

THURS _____

FRI _____

SAT _____

SUN _____

MY GOALS FOR THE WEEK

_____ ☐

_____ ☐

_____ ☐

_____ ☐

_____ ☐

MY AFFIRMATION FOR THE WEEK

WHAT I DID WELL THIS WEEK

WHAT I'D LIKE TO WORK ON NEXT WEEK

WEEKLY JOURNAL

Don't overthink it. Just write

If you're struggling, here's a prompt to get you started:

Are you living authentically? If not, what's stopping you?

W/C

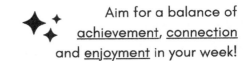
Aim for a balance of
<u>achievement</u>, <u>connection</u>
and <u>enjoyment</u> in your week!

SELF CARE PLANNER

Carving out time for yourself everyday is the key to sustained
spiritual self care. What will you do for <u>you</u> this week?

MON _____

TUES _____

WEDS _____

THURS _____

FRI _____

SAT _____

SUN _____

MY GOALS FOR THE WEEK

_____ ☐

_____ ☐

_____ ☐

_____ ☐

_____ ☐

MY AFFIRMATION FOR THE WEEK

WHAT I DID WELL THIS WEEK

WHAT I'D LIKE TO WORK ON NEXT WEEK

WEEKLY JOURNAL

Don't overthink it. Just write
If you're struggling, here's a prompt to get you started:
What is one thing you would change about yourself?

W/C _____

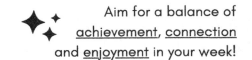

Aim for a balance of
<u>achievement</u>, <u>connection</u>
and <u>enjoyment</u> in your week!

SELF CARE PLANNER

Carving out time for yourself everyday is the key to sustained
spiritual self care. What will you do for <u>you</u> this week?

MON _____

TUES _____

WEDS _____

THURS _____

FRI _____

SAT _____

SUN _____

MY GOALS
FOR THE WEEK

_____ ☐

_____ ☐

_____ ☐

_____ ☐

_____ ☐

MY AFFIRMATION
FOR THE WEEK

WHAT I DID WELL
THIS WEEK

WHAT I'D LIKE TO WORK
ON NEXT WEEK

WEEKLY JOURNAL

Don't overthink it. Just write
If you're struggling, here's a prompt to get you started:
What is your biggest fear in life?

W/C

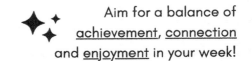

Aim for a balance of
<u>achievement</u>, <u>connection</u>
and <u>enjoyment</u> in your week!

SELF CARE PLANNER

Carving out time for yourself everyday is the key to sustained spiritual self care. What will you do for <u>you</u> this week?

MON _____

TUES _____

WEDS _____

THURS _____

FRI _____

SAT _____

SUN _____

MY GOALS
FOR THE WEEK

_____ ☐

_____ ☐

_____ ☐

_____ ☐

_____ ☐

MY AFFIRMATION
FOR THE WEEK

WHAT I DID WELL
THIS WEEK

WHAT I'D LIKE TO WORK
ON NEXT WEEK

WEEKLY JOURNAL

Don't overthink it. Just write
If you're struggling, here's a prompt to get you started:
What do you believe in?

W/C

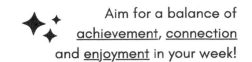

Aim for a balance of
<u>achievement</u>, <u>connection</u>
and <u>enjoyment</u> in your week!

SELF CARE PLANNER

Carving out time for yourself everyday is the key to sustained
spiritual self care. What will you do for <u>you</u> this week?

MON _____

TUES _____

WEDS _____

THURS _____

FRI _____

SAT _____

SUN _____

MY GOALS
FOR THE WEEK

_____ ☐

_____ ☐

_____ ☐

_____ ☐

_____ ☐

MY AFFIRMATION
FOR THE WEEK

WHAT I DID WELL
THIS WEEK

WHAT I'D LIKE TO WORK
ON NEXT WEEK

WEEKLY JOURNAL

Don't overthink it. Just write
If you're struggling, here's a prompt to get you started:
What does your perfect day look like?

W/C

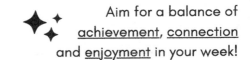

Aim for a balance of
<u>achievement</u>, <u>connection</u>
and <u>enjoyment</u> in your week!

SELF CARE PLANNER

Carving out time for yourself everyday is the key to sustained
spiritual self care. What will you do for <u>you</u> this week?

MON _____

TUES _____

WEDS _____

THURS _____

FRI _____

SAT _____

SUN _____

MY GOALS
FOR THE WEEK

_____ ☐

_____ ☐

_____ ☐

_____ ☐

_____ ☐

MY AFFIRMATION
FOR THE WEEK

WHAT I DID WELL
THIS WEEK

WHAT I'D LIKE TO WORK
ON NEXT WEEK

WEEKLY JOURNAL

Don't overthink it. Just write
If you're struggling, here's a prompt to get you started:
How do you measure success?

W/C _____

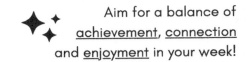

SELF CARE PLANNER

Carving out time for yourself everyday is the key to sustained spiritual self care. What will you do for <u>you</u> this week?

MON _____

TUES _____

WEDS _____

THURS _____

FRI _____

SAT _____

SUN _____

MY GOALS FOR THE WEEK

_____ ☐

_____ ☐

_____ ☐

_____ ☐

_____ ☐

MY AFFIRMATION FOR THE WEEK

WHAT I DID WELL THIS WEEK

WHAT I'D LIKE TO WORK ON NEXT WEEK

WEEKLY JOURNAL

Don't overthink it. Just write

If you're struggling, here's a prompt to get you started:

Where do you see yourself in 20 years?

W/C _____

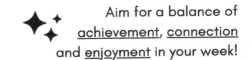

SELF CARE PLANNER

Carving out time for yourself everyday is the key to sustained spiritual self care. What will you do for <u>you</u> this week?

MON _____

TUES _____

WEDS _____

THURS _____

FRI _____

SAT _____

SUN _____

MY GOALS FOR THE WEEK

_____ ☐

_____ ☐

_____ ☐

_____ ☐

_____ ☐

MY AFFIRMATION FOR THE WEEK

WHAT I DID WELL THIS WEEK

WHAT I'D LIKE TO WORK ON NEXT WEEK

WEEKLY JOURNAL

Don't overthink it. Just write

If you're struggling, here's a prompt to get you started:

What undesirable emotions do you feel often?

W/C
_____

SELF CARE PLANNER

Carving out time for yourself everyday is the key to sustained spiritual self care. What will you do for <u>you</u> this week?

Aim for a balance of <u>achievement</u>, <u>connection</u> and <u>enjoyment</u> in your week!

MON _____

TUES _____

WEDS _____

THURS _____

FRI _____

SAT _____

SUN _____

MY GOALS FOR THE WEEK

_____ ☐

_____ ☐

_____ ☐

_____ ☐

_____ ☐

MY AFFIRMATION FOR THE WEEK

WHAT I DID WELL THIS WEEK

WHAT I'D LIKE TO WORK ON NEXT WEEK

WEEKLY JOURNAL

Don't overthink it. Just write
If you're struggling, here's a prompt to get you started:
What is your biggest priority?

W/C _____

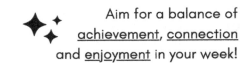

SELF CARE PLANNER

Carving out time for yourself everyday is the key to sustained spiritual self care. What will you do for <u>you</u> this week?

MON _____

TUES _____

WEDS _____

THURS _____

FRI _____

SAT _____

SUN _____

MY GOALS
FOR THE WEEK

_____ ☐

_____ ☐

_____ ☐

_____ ☐

_____ ☐

MY AFFIRMATION
FOR THE WEEK

WHAT I DID WELL
THIS WEEK

WHAT I'D LIKE TO WORK
ON NEXT WEEK

WEEKLY JOURNAL

Don't overthink it. Just write
If you're struggling, here's a prompt to get you started:
What motives you to want to improve?

_____
_____
_____
_____
_____
_____
_____
_____
_____
_____
_____
_____
_____
_____
_____
_____
_____
_____
_____
_____
_____
_____
_____

W/C

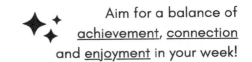

SELF CARE PLANNER

Carving out time for yourself everyday is the key to sustained spiritual self care. What will you do for <u>you</u> this week?

MON _____

TUES _____

WEDS _____

THURS _____

FRI _____

SAT _____

SUN _____

MY GOALS FOR THE WEEK

_____ ☐

_____ ☐

_____ ☐

_____ ☐

_____ ☐

MY AFFIRMATION FOR THE WEEK

WHAT I DID WELL THIS WEEK

WHAT I'D LIKE TO WORK ON NEXT WEEK

WEEKLY JOURNAL

Don't overthink it. Just write
If you're struggling, here's a prompt to get you started:
What do you think the purpose of life is?

W/C

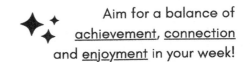
Aim for a balance of
<u>achievement</u>, <u>connection</u>
and <u>enjoyment</u> in your week!

SELF CARE PLANNER

Carving out time for yourself everyday is the key to sustained spiritual self care. What will you do for <u>you</u> this week?

MON _____

TUES _____

WEDS _____

THURS _____

FRI _____

SAT _____

SUN _____

MY GOALS
FOR THE WEEK

_____ ☐

_____ ☐

_____ ☐

_____ ☐

_____ ☐

MY AFFIRMATION
FOR THE WEEK

WHAT I DID WELL
THIS WEEK

WHAT I'D LIKE TO WORK
ON NEXT WEEK

WEEKLY JOURNAL

Don't overthink it. Just write
If you're struggling, here's a prompt to get you started:
What harsh truths do you prefer to ignore?

W/C

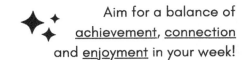
Aim for a balance of <u>achievement</u>, <u>connection</u> and <u>enjoyment</u> in your week!

SELF CARE PLANNER

Carving out time for yourself everyday is the key to sustained spiritual self care. What will you do for <u>you</u> this week?

MON _____

TUES _____

WEDS _____

THURS _____

FRI _____

SAT _____

SUN _____

MY GOALS
FOR THE WEEK

_____ ☐

_____ ☐

_____ ☐

_____ ☐

_____ ☐

MY AFFIRMATION
FOR THE WEEK

WHAT I DID WELL
THIS WEEK

WHAT I'D LIKE TO WORK
ON NEXT WEEK

WEEKLY JOURNAL

Don't overthink it. Just write
If you're struggling, here's a prompt to get you started:
What makes you excited about life?

W/C

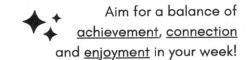

SELF CARE PLANNER

Carving out time for yourself everyday is the key to sustained spiritual self care. What will you do for <u>you</u> this week?

MON _____

TUES _____

WEDS _____

THURS _____

FRI _____

SAT _____

SUN _____

MY GOALS FOR THE WEEK

_____ ☐

_____ ☐

_____ ☐

_____ ☐

_____ ☐

MY AFFIRMATION FOR THE WEEK

WHAT I DID WELL THIS WEEK

WHAT I'D LIKE TO WORK ON NEXT WEEK

WEEKLY JOURNAL

Don't overthink it. Just write
If you're struggling, here's a prompt to get you started:
What *does professional success look like to you?*

W/C

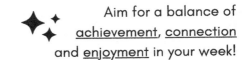

Aim for a balance of <u>achievement</u>, <u>connection</u> and <u>enjoyment</u> in your week!

SELF CARE PLANNER

Carving out time for yourself everyday is the key to sustained spiritual self care. What will you do for <u>you</u> this week?

MON _____

TUES _____

WEDS _____

THURS _____

FRI _____

SAT _____

SUN _____

MY GOALS FOR THE WEEK

MY AFFIRMATION FOR THE WEEK

WHAT I DID WELL THIS WEEK

WHAT I'D LIKE TO WORK ON NEXT WEEK

WEEKLY JOURNAL

Don't overthink it. Just write
If you're struggling, here's a prompt to get you started:
What is freedom to you?

W/C

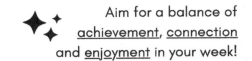

SELF CARE PLANNER

Carving out time for yourself everyday is the key to sustained spiritual self care. What will you do for <u>you</u> this week?

MON _____

TUES _____

WEDS _____

THURS _____

FRI _____

SAT _____

SUN _____

MY GOALS FOR THE WEEK

_____ ☐

_____ ☐

_____ ☐

_____ ☐

_____ ☐

MY AFFIRMATION FOR THE WEEK

WHAT I DID WELL THIS WEEK

WHAT I'D LIKE TO WORK ON NEXT WEEK

WEEKLY JOURNAL

Don't overthink it. Just write

If you're struggling, here's a prompt to get you started:

What can you do today that you weren't capable of a year ago?

W/C

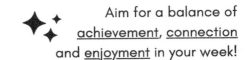

SELF CARE PLANNER

Carving out time for yourself everyday is the key to sustained spiritual self care. What will you do for <u>you</u> this week?

MON _____

TUES _____

WEDS _____

THURS _____

FRI _____

SAT _____

SUN _____

MY GOALS FOR THE WEEK

_____ ☐

_____ ☐

_____ ☐

_____ ☐

_____ ☐

MY AFFIRMATION FOR THE WEEK

WHAT I DID WELL THIS WEEK

WHAT I'D LIKE TO WORK ON NEXT WEEK

WEEKLY JOURNAL

Don't overthink it. Just write
If you're struggling, here's a prompt to get you started:
What is your biggest regret? Have you forgiven yourself?

W/C

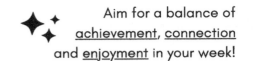
Aim for a balance of
<u>achievement</u>, <u>connection</u>
and <u>enjoyment</u> in your week!

SELF CARE PLANNER

Carving out time for yourself everyday is the key to sustained spiritual self care. What will you do for <u>you</u> this week?

MON _____

TUES _____

WEDS _____

THURS _____

FRI _____

SAT _____

SUN _____

MY GOALS
FOR THE WEEK

_____ ☐

_____ ☐

_____ ☐

_____ ☐

_____ ☐

MY AFFIRMATION
FOR THE WEEK

WHAT I DID WELL
THIS WEEK

WHAT I'D LIKE TO WORK
ON NEXT WEEK

WEEKLY JOURNAL

Don't overthink it. Just write
If you're struggling, here's a prompt to get you started:
Where does your happiness come from?

W/C _____

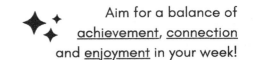

Aim for a balance of
<u>achievement</u>, <u>connection</u>
and <u>enjoyment</u> in your week!

SELF CARE PLANNER

Carving out time for yourself everyday is the key to sustained
spiritual self care. What will you do for <u>you</u> this week?

MON _____

TUES _____

WEDS _____

THURS _____

FRI _____

SAT _____

SUN _____

MY GOALS
FOR THE WEEK

_____ ☐

_____ ☐

_____ ☐

_____ ☐

_____ ☐

MY AFFIRMATION
FOR THE WEEK

WHAT I DID WELL
THIS WEEK

WHAT I'D LIKE TO WORK
ON NEXT WEEK

WEEKLY JOURNAL

Don't overthink it. Just write
If you're struggling, here's a prompt to get you started:
What does love mean to you?

W/C

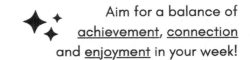

SELF CARE PLANNER

Carving out time for yourself everyday is the key to sustained spiritual self care. What will you do for <u>you</u> this week?

MON _____

TUES _____

WEDS _____

THURS _____

FRI _____

SAT _____

SUN _____

MY GOALS
FOR THE WEEK

_____ ☐

_____ ☐

_____ ☐

_____ ☐

_____ ☐

MY AFFIRMATION
FOR THE WEEK

WHAT I DID WELL
THIS WEEK

WHAT I'D LIKE TO WORK
ON NEXT WEEK

WEEKLY JOURNAL

Don't overthink it. Just write
If you're struggling, here's a prompt to get you started:
Do your personal circumstances have power over you?

W/C

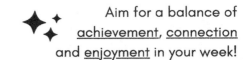

Aim for a balance of
<u>achievement</u>, <u>connection</u>
and <u>enjoyment</u> in your week!

SELF CARE PLANNER

Carving out time for yourself everyday is the key to sustained
spiritual self care. What will you do for <u>you</u> this week?

MON _____

TUES _____

WEDS _____

THURS _____

FRI _____

SAT _____

SUN _____

**MY GOALS
FOR THE WEEK**

_____ ☐

_____ ☐

_____ ☐

_____ ☐

_____ ☐

**MY AFFIRMATION
FOR THE WEEK**

**WHAT I DID WELL
THIS WEEK**

**WHAT I'D LIKE TO WORK
ON NEXT WEEK**

WEEKLY JOURNAL

Don't overthink it. Just write
If you're struggling, here's a prompt to get you started:
What limiting beliefs do you cling to?

W/C

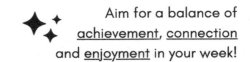

SELF CARE PLANNER

Carving out time for yourself everyday is the key to sustained spiritual self care. What will you do for <u>you</u> this week?

MON _____

TUES _____

WEDS _____

THURS _____

FRI _____

SAT _____

SUN _____

MY GOALS FOR THE WEEK

_____ ☐

_____ ☐

_____ ☐

_____ ☐

_____ ☐

MY AFFIRMATION FOR THE WEEK

WHAT I DID WELL THIS WEEK

WHAT I'D LIKE TO WORK ON NEXT WEEK

WEEKLY JOURNAL

Don't overthink it. Just write
If you're struggling, here's a prompt to get you started:
How connected do you feel to your surroundings?

W/C _____

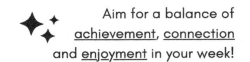

SELF CARE PLANNER

Carving out time for yourself everyday is the key to sustained spiritual self care. What will you do for <u>you</u> this week?

MON _____

TUES _____

WEDS _____

THURS _____

FRI _____

SAT _____

SUN _____

MY GOALS
FOR THE WEEK

_____ ☐

_____ ☐

_____ ☐

_____ ☐

_____ ☐

MY AFFIRMATION
FOR THE WEEK

WHAT I DID WELL
THIS WEEK

WHAT I'D LIKE TO WORK
ON NEXT WEEK

WEEKLY JOURNAL

Don't overthink it. Just write
If you're struggling, here's a prompt to get you started:
Are you here, in the present moment?

W/C _____

Aim for a balance of
achievement, connection
and enjoyment in your week!

SELF CARE PLANNER

Carving out time for yourself everyday is the key to sustained spiritual self care. What will you do for you this week?

MON _____

TUES _____

WEDS _____

THURS _____

FRI _____

SAT _____

SUN _____

MY GOALS
FOR THE WEEK

_____ ☐

_____ ☐

_____ ☐

_____ ☐

_____ ☐

MY AFFIRMATION
FOR THE WEEK

WHAT I DID WELL
THIS WEEK

WHAT I'D LIKE TO WORK
ON NEXT WEEK

WEEKLY JOURNAL

Don't overthink it. Just write
If you're struggling, here's a prompt to get you started:
Describe the best feeling you've ever experienced

_____

_____

_____

_____

_____

_____

_____

_____

_____

_____

_____

_____

_____

_____

_____

_____

_____

_____

_____

_____

_____

_____

_____

_____

_____

_____

_____

_____

W/C

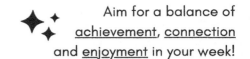

SELF CARE PLANNER

Carving out time for yourself everyday is the key to sustained spiritual self care. What will you do for <u>you</u> this week?

MON _____

TUES _____

WEDS _____

THURS _____

FRI _____

SAT _____

SUN _____

MY GOALS
FOR THE WEEK

_____ ☐

_____ ☐

_____ ☐

_____ ☐

_____ ☐

MY AFFIRMATION
FOR THE WEEK

WHAT I DID WELL
THIS WEEK

WHAT I'D LIKE TO WORK
ON NEXT WEEK

W/C

WEEKLY JOURNAL

Don't overthink it. Just write
If you're struggling, here's a prompt to get you started:
Are you holding yourself back?

W/C

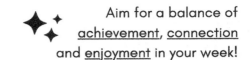
Aim for a balance of
<u>achievement</u>, <u>connection</u>
and <u>enjoyment</u> in your week!

SELF CARE PLANNER

Carving out time for yourself everyday is the key to sustained spiritual self care. What will you do for <u>you</u> this week?

MON _____

TUES _____

WEDS _____

THURS _____

FRI _____

SAT _____

SUN _____

MY GOALS
FOR THE WEEK

_____ ☐

_____ ☐

_____ ☐

_____ ☐

_____ ☐

MY AFFIRMATION
FOR THE WEEK

WHAT I DID WELL
THIS WEEK

WHAT I'D LIKE TO WORK
ON NEXT WEEK

W/C _____

WEEKLY JOURNAL

Don't overthink it. Just write
If you're struggling, here's a prompt to get you started:
How connected do you feel to your inner self?

_____
_____
_____
_____
_____
_____
_____
_____
_____
_____
_____
_____
_____
_____
_____
_____
_____
_____
_____
_____
_____
_____
_____
_____
_____
_____
_____
_____

W/C

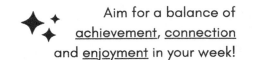

Aim for a balance of
<u>achievement</u>, <u>connection</u>
and <u>enjoyment</u> in your week!

SELF CARE PLANNER

Carving out time for yourself everyday is the key to sustained
spiritual self care. What will you do for <u>you</u> this week?

MON _____

TUES _____

WEDS _____

THURS _____

FRI _____

SAT _____

SUN _____

**MY GOALS
FOR THE WEEK**

_____ ☐

_____ ☐

_____ ☐

_____ ☐

_____ ☐

**MY AFFIRMATION
FOR THE WEEK**

**WHAT I DID WELL
THIS WEEK**

**WHAT I'D LIKE TO WORK
ON NEXT WEEK**

WEEKLY JOURNAL

Don't overthink it. Just write
If you're struggling, here's a prompt to get you started:
Have you truly accepted yourself?

SELF CARE ASSESSMENT

Congratulations on making it through 52 weeks of spiritual self care!
Have you noticed an improvement since your self care assessment in the
beginning? Complete the assessment and find new areas you'd like to
focus your attention

1 = Never   2 = Rarely   3 = Sometimes   4 = Often

	1	2	3	4
I practiced prayer or meditation	◯	◯	◯	◯
I took time for personal reflection (e.g. journalling)	◯	◯	◯	◯
I spent time in nature	◯	◯	◯	◯
I engaged in non-work / school related hobbies	◯	◯	◯	◯
I connected with others	◯	◯	◯	◯
I made time to read / listen to things that inspire me	◯	◯	◯	◯
I focused on being present in the here-and-now	◯	◯	◯	◯
I expressed my creativity (e.g. art, cooking, dancing)	◯	◯	◯	◯
I have practiced gratitude	◯	◯	◯	◯

 While you ideally want to be practising each self care behavior often, but don't worry if you aren't. Remember to be kind to yourself. Your journey is just beginning!

EMERGENCY SELF CARE TOOLKIT

RESOURCES

National Institute for Mental Health
www.nimh.nih.gov

MentalHealth.gov:
www.mentalhealth.gov

National Suicide Prevention Lifeline:
1-800-273-8255 (TALK)

Therapy for Black Girls Directory:
providers.therapyforblackgirls.com

MY SUPPORT SYSTEM

NAME: _____
EMAIL: _____
NUMBER: _____

NAME: _____
EMAIL: _____
NUMBER: _____

NAME: _____
EMAIL: _____
NUMBER: _____

TIPS FOR CHALLENGING TIMES

- **Do something that gives you pleasure**. Focus on the small pleasures of your day such as your morning coffee or walk in the park. Anything small and achieveable will do. Prioritize that moment in your day and spend that time focusing specifically on the feelings of pleasure it gives you

- To combat feelings of powerlessness commonly experienced in challenging times, **take action**, no matter how small. This could be something like making a doctor's appointment or calling a friend.

- **Take time to breathe**. Find a quiet space wherever you are and take ten deep breaths, focusing on your body. Repeat this until you feel more grounded and relaxed. This will help you to focus on the here-and-now rather than becoming consumed with negative thoughts

DID YOU ENJOY THIS BOOK? CHECK OUT OUR OTHERS

SELF CARE WORKBOOK FOR BLACK WOMEN

A 160+ page activity book covering mental, physical, spiritual and emotional self help practices. Complete with a 12-month planner and guided journal

EMOTIONAL SELF CARE FOR BLACK WOMEN

A self help activity book to address the thoughts, beliefs and triggers which affect your emotions and behavior

THE MENTAL HEALTH MIXTAPE FOR BLACK MEN

A workbook to help Black men develop coping skills and self care strategies to keep their mental health on track

**Stress Less Press are a Black-owned independent publisher.
If you enjoy this book, please consider supporting us by leaving a review on Amazon!**

WANT TO CONTINUE YOUR SELF CARE JOURNEY?

HEAD TO OUR WEBSITE AND DOWNLOAD YOUR FREE WORKSHEETS. SCAN THE QR CODE BELOW OR VISIT WWW.STRESSLESSPRESS.COM

stress less
PRESS

| stresslesspress.com

Made in the USA
Coppell, TX
22 March 2023

14632439R00063